It's a Dog's Life

BY Susan E. Goodman

ILLUSTRATED BY
David Slonim

HOW Man's Best Friend SEES, HEARS, and SMELLS the World

Flash Point

Roaring Brook Press
New York

Pssst, kid! Over here!

Do you like dogs? Sure you do. We're man's best friend, right?

But how many of your other best friends lick your face? Lick themselves? Or roll in dead animals?

You say, "Good dog!"
We wag our tails.

You say, "Stop chewing my shoe!"
We wag our tails.
What are we trying to tell you?

And what are we doing when we sniff you ALL OVER?
The truth is—dogs have a secret life.
You might as well learn about it. We're gonna be together for a long, long time.

Back in the beginning, humans thought *they* did the taming. But we also had a hand in it—a paw, anyway. We were tired of working so hard to find food. Do you think it's easy chasing down wild pigs or searching for scraps of mammoth meat some saber-toothed cat left behind? Who wouldn't want a better life?

Luckily, early humans made it easy for us. They'd toss aside tasty bones and guts left over from their dinner.

So we helped ourselves. Then, when strangers came around, of course we barked at 'em. We were thinking, "This is OUR food, OUR turf." It turns out the humans were thinking, *Ah, a garbage disposal that doubles as a watchdog.*

And that was the start of a beautiful friendship.

Bark and eat garbage—we were perfectly satisfied with this deal.

But then people began to farm and build towns. Next thing we knew, there were a lot of new jobs for us to do. So many different ones that humans gave us a major makeover.

They introduced big daddy dogs to immense mamas so their pups would be as big or bigger. And speedy mothers to fast fathers so their pups could run like the wind. Short-legged dads to stumpy moms . . . well, you get the idea.

A lot of matchmaking, a lot of change. Over hundreds and thousands of years, we all got the right size, shape, color, and skills for our new work.

There were dogs that helped humans hunt by pointing at the game or tracking it or bringing it back . . .

← Irish Setter

Beagle

Basset Hound

← Golden Retriever

dogs that fought or guarded your home and you . . .

Doberman Pinscher

Bull Mastiff

← Lhasa Apso

Dalmation

dogs that herded sheep or cattle . . .

Old English Sheepdog

Border Collie

Pembroke Welsh Corgi

dogs that hauled heavy loads . . .

Alaskan Malamute

Siberian Husky

Samoyed

dogs that got rid of pests for you—
hunting rats and snakes or chasing
rabbits and badgers down their holes . . .

Schnauzer

Airedale

Dachshund

and some of us bred simply to be your buddies.

Pug

Not all dogs fall into a convenient breed. Some dogs are mixed with a bit of this and that. Some people call us mutts—but don't think that's an insult. We can have the best traits of many different breeds, the best of D-O-G in us.

Mutts →

Whether mutts or thoroughbreds, some of us still pull sleds across Alaska and help cowboys round up cattle. But others have moved into modern times. We hunt down criminals. We patrol airports, sniffing out dangerous or smuggled goods.

German Shepherd

We alert the deaf to ringing telephones and guide the blind.

Mostly, we hang out with you. Okay, I admit it; we take this best friend business very seriously.

Even though we share your couch and your dinner (if we're lucky!), we don't really see eye-to-eye. Or, hear ear-to-ear.

For example, you humans always say the same thing on nighttime walks. "Such a beautiful evening, so peaceful and still."

Are you guys deaf?

Fact is, we hear lots of sounds that are just too high for you to make out. You're admiring the peace and quiet, while we're listening to bats screeching through the sky. You should be glad you can't hear them. They're as loud as jackhammers.

And when you practice the violin, you only hear the part of each sound that falls within your range of hearing. We suffer through all the really high parts. Trust me, you would howl too!

We hear a greater number of sounds—and we hear them *better* too. Wanna know my favorite trick? I perk up my ears and run to the window. When Dad comes home from work a few minutes later, my human family thinks I'm a genius. Don't tell 'em that I just recognized the sound of his car. And heard it four times farther away than they did.

Human's-eye View

Okay, we don't have the greatest eyesight in the world; we're not the best at seeing details. But if there's even a hint of movement, we're on it! Sheepdogs pick up their shepherd's hand signals a half-mile away.

As for all those fancy colors, who cares? In the old days—before our meals

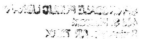

Dog's-eye View

came in a bowl—we hunted at dawn and dusk. We didn't need to see reds and oranges and greens like daytime hunters—cheetahs, say, or you humans.

Don't feel sorry for us. We've got something better. Come get a whiff of our world . . .

As far as noses are concerned, yours stink—compared to ours, that is. No wonder you're always *looking* for your sneakers instead of just *smelling* them under your bed. Or asking, "Have you seen my lunchbox?" Believe me, we know where *that* is!

Humans have 5 million special cells in their noses that detect smells. The average dog has about 220 million. A bloodhound could track you down by your scent. Even if you wore shoes. Even if you hopped onto a bicycle. Even if you left four days before. Even if you traveled 100 miles.

We use our super snouts to decode a language you'll never get a whiff of. We pee on every rock and tree for good reason. Think of that telephone pole as a newspaper or pee-mail.

If you lean down, you smell urine. *We* smell information. It's our way of finding out what's going on in the neighborhood. We even have a special organ in our nose that lets us know which dogs are around, how old they are, and how they're feeling. And if they're female, it lets us know whether or not they want to have puppies!

We sniff our way through the local canine news. Then we add our own, the higher the better, for us guys anyway. We lift our legs to get our message at nose level. We're also trying to win the "top dog" contest. That's why some half-pints jump while they're peeing. They're just trying to stay in the game.

Peeing, growling, wagging our tails—we've got plenty of ways to understand each other. We've even learned the meaning behind many of your barks—Come, Sit, Stay, even *Leave that alone!* Truth is, we may not always understand, but we do listen, which is usually enough to make you happy.

But what about you? How hard do you try to learn our language?

The Woof/English Dictionary

Fast barks: "Come on guys, check this out!"

Low, slow, and steady barks: "Who's that? I'm worried!"

Soft, low growl: "Get out of here. I mean business."

Low growl-bark: "I'll fight if you make me, but I don't really want to."

Single, sharp bark: "Hey! You stepped on my foot." "Ouch! Stop pulling out those burrs!"

Long h-o-w-l-l: "I'm here, I live here, and this is mine." Or "What do you mean leaving without me?" Or "It's *Sing-along with Sirens* time!"

Soft whimper: "Ouch, ouch, ouch." Or "That's really scary."

Panting: "Can we go already? Come on, let's go!" "This makes me so nervous!" Or "It just doesn't get any better than this!" Or "Wow, am I hot!"

That's just the vocal part of our language. We use more than barks to communicate. You've got to understand our moves to know what we're saying.

Take tail-wagging. Humans always assume we're happy. We may be saying: "I'm glad to see you" or "I don't like you;" "I'm excited" or "I'm nervous;" "I want to play" or "Watch out, I'm getting mad."

We use our whole body to get our message across.

Dogs don't have much trouble understanding each other. When we were wild, we lived in packs. We hunted together, ate together, slept together, walked, ran, and hung out together. We think of our human families as packs too. That's why we always want to eat with you, sleep with you, walk, run . . . catch my drift?

People like to think they are all equal—we don't. We want a leader to run the show. Secret is, we're happy when you're Top Dog. You get to sit wherever you want, eat first, decide where we go. And we don't have to worry—someone's in charge, keeping us safe.

That's our first choice. But if you don't step up, we will take on the job.

Look, I'm not going to give away all our secrets. But here are a few more questions my friends and I are willing to answer.

Why do most dogs eat standing up?

Theory is, we used to hunt in groups and had to protect our food from our pack-mates. Or grab theirs and run. It's tough to do either when you're lying down.

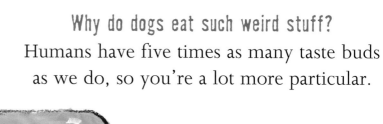

Why do dogs eat such weird stuff?

Humans have five times as many taste buds as we do, so you're a lot more particular.

Can you teach an old dog new tricks?

Sure, just be patient. Or, make it worth our while.

Why do dogs like to roll in gross stuff?

Humans wear perfume, why shouldn't we?

Why do dogs like to stick their heads out of car windows?

It's not the scenery! Our sense of smell works even better when we're moving fast. We're checking out a world of yum at 30 miles an hour.

All right kid, that's enough for now. You might wonder why I bothered to tell you *anything*.

I figured that if you know a little more about us, maybe you'll stop trying to turn us into humans. That's right, no more doggy Halloween costumes or nail polish at the groomers. And no more plaid sweaters!

I've got a better idea. Dogs are loyal, eager to please, and always ready to play.

Why don't you try being more like us?

And here's a human point of view ...

How It All Began

Dogs share a common ancestor. An ancient type of wolf was slowly tamed and bred into man's best friend.

Some scientists think this partnership with people started as far back as 100,000 years ago. Most believe the date is closer to 14,000 or 15,000 years ago.

Since they no longer needed to hunt and kill big prey, dogs gradually developed smaller skulls and teeth.

Welcome to Woofland

All dogs belong to the same species. That means that two dogs of any breed could get together and have pups (in theory, even a dachshund and a St. Bernard!).

About 400 breeds are listed in different international organizations, but the American Kennel Club only recognizes 158 of them.

The most popular purebreds are Labrador retrievers, Yorkshire terriers, German shepherds, golden retrievers, beagles, boxers, dachshunds, poodles, shih tzus, and bulldogs.

According to Guinness World Records, the smallest dog in the world is a female Chihuahua, who is 6 inches long from her nose to the tip of her tail. The tallest is a Great Dane, who is just over 42 inches high.

Specialty Jobs for Dogs

Dogs have been trained to sniff out many things from drugs and endangered species smuggled through airports to people buried in avalanches. Some dogs can even detect cancer in humans by its smell.

Around 4,000 dogs served in the Vietnam War, saving the lives of about 10,000 U.S. soldiers.

Some hotels hire dogs to sniff out bedbugs in their guestrooms. Others have "loaner" dogs for guests who miss their own pets.

Dogs in film and television have hair and makeup artists. The *New York Times* reports that Jack Russell terriers often appear in comedies and Newfoundlands play in romantic films.

Friends Forever

Almost 75 million pet dogs live in the United States. That's about one dog for every four people.

Some Egyptian pharaohs loved their pets so much, they mummified the dogs to accompany them in their tombs.

Having a dog is good for you. You get more exercise. On average, people who have a dog (or cat) live longer than those who don't.

They might help you become smarter too. One study shows that kids who have pets miss fewer days of school.

What Dogs Hear

We have nine muscles in our ears that barely work. Dogs have seventeen muscles that all work perfectly. Those muscles prick up dogs' ears and move them around to catch any sound. That's one reason why dogs hear better than we do.

China and Japan use dogs (and other animals) to help predict earthquakes. Scientists think that dogs act nervous right before a quake because they hear sounds we cannot hear.

Many dogs run from vacuum cleaners because they make a loud, high-pitched shrieking sound that we can't hear.

What Dogs See

Dogs don't see many of the colors we do. They get a lot of their information from other cues, such as smell, texture, brightness, and position. A seeing-eye dog cannot see red. But he knows a traffic light is red when the top light is brighter than the others.

Dogs see very well at dawn and dusk. Their eyes have a special layer that reflects light so that the eye can reabsorb the rays. That reflective layer is what makes a dog's eyes shine in the dark.

People's eyes are better at measuring distance. But dogs have a wider field of vision, which means they can see more of what's going on at the sides of their heads.

What Dogs Smell

Some experts think a dog's sense of smell is 1,000 to 10,000 times better than ours. If a scent you could smell in a normal room was spread out evenly, a dog could smell it in a room two-and-a-half miles wide and two-and-a-half miles long.

The section of a dog's brain devoted to smell is forty times bigger than in human ones.

The moisture on dogs' noses works like glue, trapping a smell so the dog can take it in.

Dogs usually hate the smell of lemon, lime, orange, and spicy scents like red pepper.

The Well-Read Dog

Free-roaming dogs spend up to three hours a day checking all the scent marks in their territory.

About 25 percent of female dogs raise a back leg to pee, but they still pee on the ground.

Of all the tricks animal trainers teach dogs for movies, getting them to raise a rear leg on command is one of the hardest.

Do You Speak Dog?

English speakers describe a dog's bark as *bow-wow*, the Spanish say *jau-jau*, Russians say *gav-gav*, the Chinese *wung-wung*.

Early dogs hunted in silence like wolves. Some of today's hunting dogs, like terriers and beagles, were bred to bark a lot while chasing prey so their humans can know where they went.

Submissive dogs often crouch and roll on their backs to look like young dogs. This body language helps them stay safe; adult dogs usually don't attack puppies.

Leader of the Pack

One way a leader maintains control is by staring into the eyes of other pack members. (Don't try this with a dog you don't know that could be aggressive.)

Since they are pack animals, dogs can get very upset when separated from their pack (which might mean you!). They can react by barking, howling, digging, and chewing.

The lead dog of a pack usually sleeps in a high place to watch the others. If you let a dog onto your bed, you're giving it the same position and status. About half of all dog owners allow their dogs to sleep on the bed with them.

Bibliography

One day I was walking in a park when a sheepdog bounded past me. I wondered how he experienced that beautiful New England fall afternoon. I knew that dogs don't see as many colors as we do. But what did he see and what did it look like? I wished I had a pair of magic glasses that gave me a dog's eye view of things. In that moment, this book was born.

To find those answers and more, I read a lot of great books about dogs. Here are some of my favorites.

Grown-up books:

Coren, Stanley. *Why Does My Dog Act that Way?* New York: Free Press, 2006.

Fogle, Bruce. *The Dog's Mind: Understanding your Dog's Behavior.* Washington, D.C.: Howell Book House, 1992.

Grandin, Temple & Catherine Johnson. *Animals in Translation: Using the Mysteries of Autism to Decode Animal Behaviour.* New York: Simon and Schuster, 2005.

Morris, Desmond. *Dogwatching.* New York: Crown Publishers, Inc., 1986.

Thurston, Mary Elizabeth. *The Lost History of the Canine Race: Our 15,000-Year Love Affair with Dogs.* Kansas City: Andrews McMeel, 1996.

Kids' nonfiction and fiction:

DiCamillo, Kate. *Because of Winn-Dixie.* Cambridge MA: Candlewick Press, 2000.

Jenkins, Steve. *Dogs and Cats.* Boston: Houghton Mifflin, 2007.

Kehret, Peg & Greg Farrar. *Shelter Dogs: Amazing Stories of Adopted Strays.* Morton Grove, IL: Albert Whitman, 1999.

Martin, Ann M. *A Dog's Life: Autobiography of a Stray.* New York: Scholastic, Inc., 2005.

Paulsen, Gary. *My Life in Dog Years.* New York: Delacorte Books for Young Readers, 1998.

Provensen, Alice. *A Day in the Life of Murphy.* New York: Simon & Schuster, 2003.

Singer, Marilyn. *A Dog's Gotta Do What a Dog's Gotta: Dogs at Work.* New York: Henry Holt & Co., 2000.

Turner, Pamela S. & Yan Nascimbene. *Hachiko: The True Story of a Loyal Dog.* Boston: Houghton Mifflin Co., 2004.

To Granddog (aka Ella)
—S.G.

To Shaggy Maggie Moo
Wagtail Slonim
—D.S.

Text copyright © 2012 by Susan Goodman
Illustrations copyright © 2012 by David Slonim
Published by Flash Point, an imprint of Roaring Brook Press
Roaring Brook Press is a division of Holtzbrinck Publishing Holdings Limited Partnership
175 Fifth Avenue, New York, New York 10010
mackids.com

Library of Congress Cataloging-in-Publication Data

Goodman, Susan E., 1952–
   It's a dog's life : how man's best friend sees, hears, and smells the world / written by Susan E. Goodman ;
illustrated by Daviv Slonim. — 1st ed.
     p.   cm.
   Includes bibliographical references.
   ISBN 978-1-59643-448-6
   1. Dogs—Juvenile literature.   2. Dogs—Juvenile humor.   3. Dogs—Evolution—Juvenile literature.
4. Dogs—Behavior—Juvenile literature.   I. Slonim, David, ill.   II. Title.
SF426.5.G655 2012
636.7—dc23

2011022965

Roaring Brook Press books are available for special promotions and premiums.
For details contact: Director of Special Markets, Holtzbrinck Publishers.

First edition 2012
Printed in China by South China Printing Co., Dongguan City, Guangdong Province

1 3 5 7 9 10 8 6 4 2